EXPLORING WORLD CULTURES

Ecuador

Lisa Idzikowski

Cavendish
Square

New York

Published in 2021 by Cavendish Square Publishing, LLC
243 5th Avenue, Suite 136, New York, NY 10016

Copyright © 2021 by Cavendish Square Publishing, LLC

First Edition

Website: cavendishsq.com

This publication represents the opinions and views of the author based on his or her personal experience, knowledge, and research. The information in this book serves as a general guide only. The author and publisher have used their best efforts in preparing this book and disclaim liability rising directly or indirectly from the use and application of this book.

All websites were available and accurate when this book was sent to press.

Library of Congress Cataloging-in-Publication Data

Names: Idzikowski, Lisa, author. | Cavendish Square Publishing LLC.
Title: Ecuador / Lisa Idzikowski.
Other titles: Exploring world cultures.
Description: First Edition. | New York : Cavendish Square Publishing, 2021.
| Series: Exploring world cultures | Includes webography.
Identifiers: LCCN 2019045433 (print) | LCCN 2019045434 (ebook) | ISBN
9781502656711 (Library Binding) | ISBN 9781502656698 (Paperback) | ISBN
9781502656728 (eBook) | ISBN 9781502656704 (Set)
Subjects: LCSH: Ecuador--Juvenile literature. | Ecuador--Description and
travel.
Classification: LCC F3708.5 .I49 2021 (print) | LCC F3708.5 (ebook) | DDC
986.6--dc23
LC record available at https://lccn.loc.gov/2019045433
LC ebook record available at https://lccn.loc.gov/2019045434

Editor: Kristen Susienka
Copy Editor: Nathan Heidelberger
Designer: Jessica Nevins

The photographs in this book are used by permission and through the courtesy of: Cover Hugh Sitton/Corbis/Getty Images Plus/Getty Images; pp. 4, 8, 20, 28 Fotos593/Shutterstock.com; pp. 5, 21, 25 ireneuke/Shutterstock.com; p. 6 pavalena/Shutterstock.com; p. 7 tunasalmon/Shutterstock.com; p. 9 Janusz Pienkowski/Shutterstock.com; p. 10 Karol Kozlowski/Shutterstock.com; p. 11 Fabricio Burbano/Shutterstock.com; p. 12 Ammit Jack/Shutterstock.com; p. 13 Jess Kraft/Shutterstock.com; p. 14 Elisa Locci/Shutterstock.com; p. 15 jarno verdonk/Shutterstock.com; p. 16 Rafal Cichawa/Shutterstock.com; p. 17 Jam Travels/Shutterstock.com; p. 18 FOTOGRIN/Shutterstock.com; p. 19 Alexandre Rotenberg/Shutterstock.com; p. 22 Kirk Hewlett/Shutterstock.com; p. 23 Omri Eliyahu/Shutterstock.com; p. 24 KalypsoWorldPhotography/Shutterstock.com; p. 26 Keeton Gale/Shutterstock.com; p. 27 Matthias Hangst/Getty Images; p. 29 AS Food studio/Shutterstock.com.

Some of the images in this book illustrate individuals who are models. The depictions do not imply actual situations or events.

CPSIA compliance information: Batch #CS20CSQ: For further information contact Cavendish Square Publishing LLC, New York, New York, at 1-877-980-4450.

Printed in the United States of America

Find us on

Contents

Introduction

Ecuador is a country in South America. It's home to many kinds of people, plants, and animals. People have lived there for thousands of years. In the past, Ecuador was

There are many cities to explore in Ecuador, like Quito, shown here.

home to different civilizations, or groups of people. One of the most famous was the Inca. Parts of temples built by the Inca can still be seen today.

Tourism brings a lot of money to Ecuador. Visitors like to ride horses, explore the forests, learn about the country's history, and see the interesting plants and animals in Ecuador.

Although it was ruled by Spain for a long time, today Ecuador is its own country. It's a fun place to learn about, so let's begin!

These Ecuadorians celebrate their country and culture, or way of life, by wearing **traditional** clothing.

The country of Ecuador sits on the coast of South America. It lies along the Pacific Ocean and is bordered by two other South American countries: Peru to the east and south and Colombia to the north.

Ecuador is made up of four main areas. One runs along the coast,

Ecuador is slightly smaller than the US state of Nevada.

FACT!

Ecuador lies on a path called the Ring of Fire that has many volcanoes. Ecuador has one of the world's highest active volcanoes, which is called Cotopaxi.

The Ring of Fire

The Ring of Fire is a path around the Pacific Ocean lined by volcanoes. This path covers about 24,900 miles (40,000 kilometers). Over 450 volcanoes are found there. Most of the world's earthquakes happen in this area too.

one is formed by mountains, and one spreads to the east beyond the mountains. The last

The Ring of Fire is shown here.

area is made up of the Galápagos Islands.

Ecuador is home to snowy mountains and rich rain forests. It also has many rivers and waterfalls.

Today, Ecuador's official name is the Republic of Ecuador. The first people in Ecuador arrived long ago. For thousands of years, they lived on the land. Different groups of **indigenous** people

Examples of Inca buildings can be seen in Ecuador.

farmed and fished. In the 1400s, one group—the Inca from Peru—took control.

However, the Inca's rule didn't last. In the 1500s, Spanish explorers came. They conquered

FACT!

Spanish explorer Francisco Pizarro and his men crushed the Inca Empire in the early 1530s.

Ecuador's George Washington

Simón Bolívar is well known in Ecuador. He was a general who battled against the rule of Spain in South America in the 1800s. He's often said to be much like another famous general, George Washington. In 1822, Bolívar and his troops won freedom for Ecuador. They also helped free other South American countries.

This picture shows what Simón Bolívar looked like.

the native people, or beat them in war, and destroyed their homes. By 1534, Spain ruled the whole area. A big change came almost 300 years later when Ecuador became independent in 1822.

VOTE ✓

The government of Ecuador has gone through many changes. Over the years, the country has been run in different ways. Today, it's a presidential republic.

Ecuador's government meets in this building, called the Carondelet Palace.

Much like the United States, it has a president who leads the country. A vice president helps out. Both serve four-year terms. They are elected by Ecuador's people.

FACT!

Quito is Ecuador's capital. It's named for the Quitu, the native people who founded the city. It lies close to the **equator**.

A written **constitution** lists many of the rules of the land. A group of elected lawmakers called the National Assembly also serves the country. The

Quito is a beautiful city, with its volcano, Cotopaxi, in the background.

National Court of Justice is the highest court in Ecuador. Other courts and judges run the system of law throughout the country.

Elections

Citizens of Ecuador ages 16 and over can vote in the country's elections. Between the ages of 18 and 65, Ecuadorians are required to vote.

The Economy

Throughout history, farming has played a starring role in Ecuador's business and trade. Today, it's still important. However, services and tourism are big parts

Tourists listen to a guide on a tour of an Ecuadorian wildlife park.

too. Over half of the working people in Ecuador have service jobs. That means they work in places like hotels, schools, stores, or hospitals. A large number of people also work at tourism companies.

FACT!

At one time, Ecuadorians used a form of money called sucres. In 2000, Ecuador chose the US dollar for its money instead.

Counting on Cacao

The cacao tree grows in Ecuador and other warm, wet areas. Chocolate is made from the seeds of this tree. Without cacao, people couldn't enjoy their favorite chocolate treats!

The seeds used for making chocolate are found inside large pods like this one. The pods grow on cacao trees.

Others work in the oil business.

Ecuador trades with many other countries. It exports, or ships, items to other places. Oil, bananas, cacao, coffee, fish, and shrimp are examples. The United States is Ecuador's top trading partner, followed by China, Colombia, and Vietnam.

13

Ecuador is rich in **biodiversity**. Plants and animals of all kinds fill its coasts, mountain ranges, and rain forests. Popular animals include giant Galápagos

Llamas are animals that live in Ecuador and other parts of South America.

tortoises, llamas, and river dolphins.

Even though it has lots of beautiful parts, Ecuador is also a place with many **environmental** problems. Forests are being cut down. Oil

FACT!

Environmental groups in Ecuador are trying to stop the sale of single-use plastics, including plastic straws.

Plastic and Pollution

Plastic garbage is washing up on the Galápagos Islands. The animals that live there are harmed when they eat it. To them, it looks like food. Caring people are trying to do something about it. They gather up the garbage. In some cases, they can recycle it.

Recycling is becoming more important in Ecuador.

companies cause pollution, and so do plastics, like plastic bags and straws. Climate change—change in the weather over a long period of time because of people—is also hurting the environment. These problems are harming many animals in Ecuador.

15

In 2019, the population of Ecuador reached over 17 million. Most of the people—64 percent—live in cities. The biggest cities are Guayaquil and Quito.

Ecuadorian women are busy at this market.

The people of Ecuador share a special history. Indigenous, Spanish, and African backgrounds combine to make up the culture seen today. Most Ecuadorians come from both Spanish and native backgrounds. Others

FACT!

Over 70 percent of Ecuadorians are mestizos. This means they have both indigenous and Spanish backgrounds.

have backgrounds from other areas of Europe or from Africa.

Over the years, many people have moved into and out of

This Ecuadorian family is posing for a photo.

Ecuador. Some people moved from Ecuador to Spain to start new lives. Today, many people from Colombia are moving to Ecuador. That's because Colombia is facing hard times.

A Hard Part of History

Starting in the 1500s, slavery was practiced in Ecuador. Black people from Africa were brought to the country to be slaves. Slavery ended in the 1850s. **Descendants** of slaves still live in the country today.

Lifestyle

Many people in Ecuador live in cities. They live in houses or apartments. Kids go to school. Many parents work outside the home. An Ecuadorian family often has two children.

Public buses are a common way of getting around in Ecuador.

Life outside of the big cities can be very different. Many indigenous people live in the country. In **rural** areas, families are more likely to be poor. They might live in houses without running

FACT!

Ninety-four percent of people in Ecuador age 15 and older can read and write.

water. Many people live on small farms where they grow their own food.

Ecuador has schools where students can learn. Children ages 6 to 14 are required to

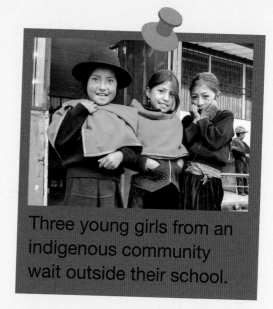

Three young girls from an indigenous community wait outside their school.

go to school. It's not always easy to get to school, especially in rural areas. Ecuador also has universities, or schools of higher learning.

Health Care in Ecuador

Everyone in Ecuador gets free health care. Ecuadorians can go to hospitals and doctors working around the country. There are 2 doctors for every 1,000 people in Ecuador.

Religion

In many countries around the world, religion—a person's belief system—is an important part of life. The same is true in Ecuador.

This church stands tall in Quito.

Most Ecuadorians follow a religion, though not all follow the same religion. The majority of people are Roman Catholic. That makes sense because it was the religion of the Spanish, who ruled Ecuador for hundreds of years. At one time, a person had

FACT!

About 8 percent of the population of Ecuador doesn't believe in any religion.

Mixing Beliefs

Some people in Ecuador practice a special type of religion that mixes Catholicism and indigenous beliefs. One of their goddesses is Mother Earth, or Pachamama. She's believed to be holy like Mary, the mother of Jesus Christ, in Roman Catholicism.

Shown here is a group of people honoring Pachamama in Ecuador.

to be a Roman Catholic to be a citizen of Ecuador. This is not true today.

Today, people in Ecuador have the right to believe in a religion of their choosing or no religion at all. Other religions practiced by Ecuador's people include Judaism, Islam, and indigenous religions.

Language

Throughout their country, Ecuadorians use three major languages: Spanish, Quechua, and Shuar. Spanish is spoken by the largest number of people—over 90 percent.

This sign for a nature park in Ecuador greets visitors in Spanish and English.

It's also the language most commonly used in government, business, religion, and education.

Quechua is the second most commonly used language. Speakers are indigenous people. Many

FACT!

The equator runs through northern Ecuador. Because of this, the country is named after the Spanish word for it, *ecuador*.

Apart from Kichwa and Shuar, about 11 more indigenous languages are spoken in Ecuador. Experts believe that one, Záparo, is about to go away forever. It's thought that only about five people still speak it.

speak a kind of Quechua called Kichwa. People who speak Kichwa often live in the south-central area of the Andes Mountains. Slightly over 4 percent of the population speaks Quechua.

Many languages can be heard in the markets of Ecuador.

Shuar is also an indigenous language. About 35,000 speakers use it. They mostly live in the southeastern part of Ecuador's rain forest.

Holidays, parades, and parties are a large part of life in Ecuador. Certain holidays, like Christmas and Easter, are religious celebrations. Others, like Labor Day and Independence Day,

A group of boys and girls dance in a parade celebrating Inti Raymi.

have nothing to do with religion. Some days of celebration come from important indigenous practices. For example, Inti Raymi honors the day when the sun is out the longest, which is called the

FACT!

Ecuador's national music style is called pasillo. It combines different Latin American rhythms to create a fun sound.

summer solstice.

Ecuadorians value folk art. Some popular examples are rugs, bags, and hats. People weave these items. They also **carve** wood and make

Men and women weave items like the scarf shown here to sell in Ecuador.

jewelry and musical instruments. Artwork like this is sold at Ecuador's markets and stores.

A Christmas Shoe!

Christmas is a time of fun traditions in Ecuador. Boys and girls make lists of presents they would like. They stuff the lists into old shoes. On Christmas morning, the children find presents left by Papa Noel, or Father Christmas.

Ecuador offers much fun for visitors and citizens. Like many people around the world, Ecuadorians enjoy soccer (called *fútbol* in Ecuador). In fact, many Ecuadorians say it's their favorite

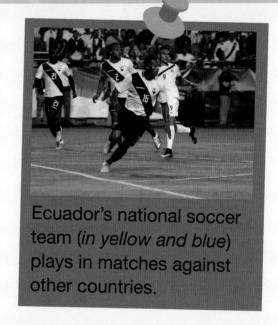

Ecuador's national soccer team (*in yellow and blue*) plays in matches against other countries.

sport. There are local teams and a national soccer team. The national team plays in Quito. Basketball, volleyball, and biking are also popular sports.

FACT!

In June 2019, Richard Carapaz became the first man from Ecuador to win the well-known Grand Tour bike race in Italy.

Ecuador and the Olympics

Ecuador has taken part in each of the Summer Olympics since 1968. The country won its first Olympic gold medal in 1996. Ecuador took part in the Winter Olympics for the first time in 2018.

Klaus Jungbluth Rodriguez holds his country's flag at the Olympics in 2018.

Families in Ecuador enjoy time together. They picnic or go to the beach. Card games keep people busy too. Kids love to run and play hide-and-seek. Some kids also play video games. Nature is a big part of life in this country, and there are many parks in Ecuador to visit.

27

Food

In Ecuador, food is made in many different ways. In the mountains, people might eat simpler foods. Near the coast, people may eat more seafood. In large cities, people

Many people in Ecuador eat *encebollado*.

might eat at restaurants or fast-food places. Often, Ecuadorian food has lots of flavor and color.

Soup is eaten at almost every meal. *Locro* is one kind of tasty soup. It's made of potatoes, cheese, corn, and sometimes meat. People also

Cuy is a meat eaten in Ecuador. It's actually roasted guinea pig!

Potatoes

Ecuadorians love potatoes. They eat all kinds. Most meals have some type of potato in them.

One way to serve a potato in Ecuador is as a *llapingacho,* or potato patty.

Potato patties are also called potato pancakes.

make stews. Both soups and stews are made with chicken, beef, goat, fish, and vegetables. *Encebollado*, or fish stew, is a national dish.

Everyone in Ecuador eats lots of rice, potatoes, beans, and fried green bananas. Ecuadorians also love to put hot sauce over meals.

Glossary

biodiversity Many kinds of plants and animals living in a certain environment.

carve To cut wood into objects using special tools.

constitution A document that explains the rules for how a government works.

descendant A person belonging to the same group or family line.

environmental Dealing with the natural world around us.

equator An invisible line around the middle of Earth where temperatures are hot and the amount of daylight is almost the same every day of the year.

indigenous Referring to the first people who lived in an area, before outside groups moved in.

rural Relating to the country, as in living outside of a city.

tourism The business of helping people from around the world travel somewhere for fun and learning.

traditional Following rules or styles from long ago.

Find Out More

Books

Lomberg, Michelle. *Ecuador.* New York, NY: AV2 by
Weigl, 2018.

Markovics, Joyce L. *Ecuador.* Minneapolis, MN:
Bearport Publishing, 2017.

Website

National Geographic Kids: Ecuador

kids.nationalgeographic.com/explore/countries/
ecuador

This website includes facts and information about
Ecuador's history, nature, geography, and more.

Video

Galápagos Islands Video

video.nationalgeographic.com/video/00000144-0a42-
d3cb-a96c-7b4f2c0e0000

This video explores Ecuador's Galápagos Islands.

Index

About the Author

Lisa Idzikowski is a biologist and writer from Milwaukee, Wisconsin. She loves science, history, and living near Lake Michigan. When she isn't reading, researching, or writing, Idzikowski works on her native plant garden to attract birds, bees, and butterflies. She hopes to someday see the wildlife of the Galápagos Islands.